Sexuality Now

What it means
And
Embracing it's
diversity

Justin Hutt

Table Of Content

Chapter one

Understanding Human sexuality

The way that humans experience and express their sexuality is known as human sexuality. This might encompass a variety of actions and identities, as well as ideas and sentiments about oneself and other people. Being sexually active is an essential component of being human, and it has a big impact on how we relate to people and interact with them. Along with causing conflict and misunderstandings, it may also be a source of joy and fulfillment. People must comprehend and respect both their own and other people's sexuality.
Human sexuality is the term used to describe how people experience and act sexually. This can encompass a variety of traits, preferences, and identities, including sexual orientation, gender identity, and sexual behavior.

Kissing, snuggling, and sexual contact is just a few examples of sexual activity. The motivations behind these acts can range from pleasure to intimacy to reproduction.

An individual's emotional, romantic, and sexual attraction to others is referred to as their sexual orientation. Being drawn to people of the same gender (homosexuality), the opposing gender (heterosexuality), or different genders is an example of this (bisexual).

The term "gender identity" refers to a person's internal sense of their gender, which may or may not coincide with the gender that was biologically given to them at birth.

Recognizing and accepting the variety of sexual experiences and manifestations among people is a necessary step in understanding human sexuality. It also entails being aware of and dealing with concerns relating to sexual health and wellness, such as controlling and preventing STDs and making complete sexual education accessible.

Our internal sense of self as being male, female, or another gender is known as gender identity. Our emotional and physical attraction to others, including those of the same gender, the opposite gender, or both, is referred to as our sexual orientation.

The methods we display our sexuality, such as through sexual action, masturbation, and sexual expression, are all included in our sexual behavior. The fantasies, cravings, and thoughts we experience regarding sexual behavior are referred to as sexual wants.

Recognizing and appreciating the variety of sexual identities and behaviors, as well as the social, cultural, and biological elements that affect sexuality, are essential to understanding human sexuality. Understanding the value of communication and consent in sexual relationships is also necessary.

Putting sexuality in context Male and female Gender: a person's identity as a man, woman, or another gender, such as transgender. Sexual behavior: conduct that elicits arousal and raises the possibility of orgasm. Religion has given humans most of their knowledge about sexuality for the vast majority of history that has been recorded. These religions have a significant influence. Science Although religious beliefs continue to have an impact on our conceptions of sexuality, the scientific study of sex began in the 19th century. A significant addition to the understanding of sex was made by Freud. There is a belief that women and men are sexual beings, and that sexual deviations from the norm are frequently innocuous. This philosophy is forced onto society. Interest in "pathological" sexuality is rising. This produced an impact that lasted a long time but is neither impartial nor forgiving. The terms heterosexuality and homosexuality, as well as masochism, pedophilia, and other related notions, were all coined. Sex research frequently crosses disciplinary boundaries. The function that religion played in earlier ages may be duplicated by the mass media in modern-day America.

The function that religion played in earlier ages may be duplicated by the mass media in modern-day America.

Three different influences from media are possible.

Cultivation
the idea that exposure to the media leads people to believe that what they see there is representative of mainstream cultural events
schedule creation

the notion that the stories that the media choose to cover determine what is noteworthy and what is not
societal education
The notion that the media presents role models for us to emulate, sometimes even unconsciously
The internet has a significant impact on mass media.
It could have both favorable and unfavorable impacts on sexual health.

Across-the-Culture Views on Sexuality

Cultural knowledge builds up through time.
Culture is the set of customary beliefs and values that are passed down through a group's generations and are communicated to its members through symbols.
Ethnocentrism frequently has an impact on how we perceive human sexual behavior.
The inclination to view one's ethnic group and culture as superior to others and to think that its traditions and way of life

should be used as the standard by which other cultures should be appraised is known as ethnocentrism.
The differences across cultures are substantial.

Though the specific restrictions vary considerably from one culture to the next, sexual behavior is regulated in some form by every society.
No civilization has thought it appropriate to completely decriminalize sexual activity, maybe out of concern that this would cause societal unrest.

Most cultures have taboos against incest.
The social taboo against having sexual relations with blood relatives is known as incest.
The majority of societies view forced sexual activity as rape.

From one community to the next, sexual behavior and views differ significantly following the laws.

Different sexual approaches

There aren't many cultures where kissing is taboo.
Additionally, there are some variations in kissing methods.
Cunnilingus: mouth-based genital stimulation in women
rather typical in our society, as well as in other societies.
In certain societies, part of the sexual practice involves hurting the other.
The frequency of sexual relations between married partners varies greatly from one culture to the next. Very few societies actively promote sexual relations at specific periods.

Instead, most societies have rules that prohibit sex outside of specific times or circumstances.
Masturbation

Masturbation is the act of stimulating one's genitalia to elicit sexual desire.
varies greatly between civilizations.
All human communities, ranging from mild criticism to harsh punishment, express some disapproval of adult masturbation.
But at least a few adults in every society seem to engage in it.

Other cultures tolerate female masturbation.

Sex that occurs before and after marriage

The laws governing premarital sex vary depending on society.
Most cultures have complex and conflicting views on extramarital sex.

The most illegal kind of sexual contact, second only to incest, is extramarital sex.
Even when it is legal, extramarital sex is still constrained by rules.

Sex with partners of the same gender

Different cultures have a wide range of perspectives on same-gender sexual expression.
Two general guidelines appear to emerge when attitudes regarding homosexuality and same-gender behavior vary greatly.

Regardless of how society views homosexuality, at least some people engage in the behavior.
In none of the societies investigated, same-gender sexual behavior never represents the majority of adult sexual behavior.

criteria for attractiveness

Physical traits play a big role in deciding who one picks as a sex partner in every human society.
The definition of attractiveness varies widely.
One norm does appear to be a universal truth: most human societies find people with dark skin unattractive.

differences by social class and ethnic group in the United States

The American culture exhibits a wide range of sexual behavior.

Social status and gender

Women are more likely to utilize the pill as a method of birth control the more educated they are.
Sexuality and social class may have mutually beneficial effects.

College students are more likely to get married after living together for the first time.

In the United States, ethnicity and sexual orientation

Numerous ethnic groups make up the population of the United States, and there are some differences in sexual behavior among these groups.
The groupings do not significantly diverge.
Only by comprehending a group's cultural background, as well as its current social and economic realities, can one comprehend the sexuality of that community.

Racial microaggressions are imperceptible, frequently unconscious insults made at individuals of color.

The importance of cross-cultural research

They help us understand the vast differences in human sexual behavior and put our ideals and actions into perspective.

These studies offer compelling proof of the influence of culture and education on how we behave sexually.

Instincts, desires, and biology do not entirely dictate how people behave sexually.

Chapter Two

Exploring Human sexuality
The way that humans experience and express their sexuality is known as human sexuality. ses, as stendens, s s. s. s. s. s. s. s. s s as s In addition to social and cultural conventions, it is influenced by a person's biological sex, gender identity, and sexual orientation. Individuals can make educated decisions regarding their sexual health and well-being by having a thorough understanding of human sexuality.

A complicated and varied component of being human is sexuality. It covers how individuals experience and express their sexuality, as well as how they engage in sexual activity with others. This can involve actions, attitudes, values, and behaviors that have an impact on sexual orientation, sexual identity, and general sexual health.

The expression and experience of sexual wants and actions are referred to as human sexuality. Sexual orientation, gender identity, sexual attraction, sexual behavior, and reproductive health are just a few of the many issues it covers.

Human sexuality is influenced by a variety of elements, including biological, psychological, social, and cultural effects. For instance, while social norms and cultural beliefs might have an impact on sexual behavior and attitudes, hormones and genetics also have an impact on sexual orientation.

Investigating human sexuality can help throw light on topics such as sexual health and well-being as well as how people create and maintain personal relationships. Additionally, it can support the acceptance of various sexual orientations and identities.

A complicated and intricate component of human life is sexuality. the as a. a.......................

The term "sexual orientation," which describes a person's emotional, romantic, and sexual attraction to others, is one of the fundamental elements of human sexuality. Heterosexual, gay, bisexual, pansexual, and asexual are among the sexual orientations.

Gender identity, which refers to a person's sense of self as male, female, or non-binary, is another crucial part of human sexuality. Individuals who identify as transgender, genderqueer, or non-binary may differ from the sex assigned at birth.

Human sexuality also includes a variety of sexual expressions and behaviors, including sex with partners, masturbation, and the use of sex toys. Additionally, it covers the study of sexual health and well-being, which covers contraception, safe sexual behavior, and the avoidance of STDs.

Individuals can better understand and manage their own sexual experiences as well as create satisfying relationships with others by investigating and understanding human sexuality. Additionally, it can aid in lessening prejudice and discrimination towards those who identify as different genders and sexual orientations.

A complicated and multidimensional component of the human experience and identity is sexuality. It covers a broad spectrum of actions, ideas, and sensations associated with sexual desire, pleasure, and intimacy. Numerous elements, such as biology, society, societal conventions, and personal experiences, can have an impact on one's sexual orientation.

Sexual orientation, gender identity, and sexual behavior are some of the most important aspects of human sexuality. An individual's emotional, romantic, and sexual attraction to others is referred to as their sexual orientation. Being heterosexual, homosexual, lesbian, bisexual, or pansexual is one example. An individual's internal perception of their gender, which may or may not correspond with the sex given to them at birth, is referred to as gender identity. The acts people take in response to feelings of sexual attraction and pleasure are referred to as sexual behavior. This can entail physical and emotional intimacy in addition to sexual activity including intercourse, oral sex, and masturbation.

Cultural and socioeconomic conventions, which can differ considerably from one country to the next, also have an impact on human sexuality. These standards have the power to influence a person's ideas on sex and relationships, as well as their behaviors and sexual expressions. An individual's sexuality can also be impacted by personal experiences, such as those from childhood, sexual trauma, and mental health problems.

Learning about the many facets of sexual identity and behavior as well as the variables that affect them can be part of exploring human sexuality. Examining the place of sexuality in society and how cultural norms and individual experiences influence it can also be part of it. In the end, studying human sexuality can help people better understand and appreciate both their sexuality and the variety of sexual orientations that exist in general.

the use of evolutionary biology to comprehend social behavior in both humans and other species.

Sociobiologists investigate the reasons for the evolution of specific sexual patterns in people.

Sociobiologists contend that many of the qualities we consider when determining attractiveness are suggestive of the person's health and vitality.

These in turn are probably connected to the individual's capacity for reproduction.

So perhaps our preoccupation with physical attractiveness is a result of natural selection and evolution.

Since attractiveness is a sign of health, it plays a bigger role in mate choice in communities where there are more ill people.

According to this theory, socializing, participating in sports, getting engaged, and other such practices are quite similar to other species' courtship rituals.

The potential couple's chance to evaluate each other's compatibility during the courtship.

If parents emotionally connect and have an attachment tendency, their child has a much better chance of surviving.

More frequent sexual encounters could result from an emotional connection. Sex's pleasurable side effects will further solidify the relationship. Parental investment is the behavior and resources parents use to help their children survive and reproduce successfully. Numerous objections to sociobiology have been raised. the determinism of life It is based on an outdated evolutionary paradigm that contemporary biologists view as simplistic. Sociobiologists believe that.

Developmental psychology

The study of psychological processes that have undergone natural selection is known as evolutionary psychology.

It is conceivable that cognitive or emotional structures also evolved in response to selection forces if behaviors did.

A guy would have a better chance of having children if he could precisely determine whether a woman was healthy and pregnant.

According to sexual strategies, short-term, or casual, mating and long-term reproduction present different adaptive challenges for males and females.

Different techniques result from these variations.

A female may select a partner in short-term mating who provides her with immediate resources, such as food or money.

A female may select a partner for long-term mating if they look to be able and willing to offer resources indefinitely.

When looking for a long-term partner, a male may choose a sexually accessible female for a brief relationship.

According to the notion, females compete with one another intrasexual to get access to men.

Evolutionary psychology criticisms

The expressed preferences for mating between men and women are remarkably comparable.

They both favor long-term plans and few, if any, short-term partners.

It presumes that any trait we see must have some sort of adaptive relevance.

There are two groups for female genitalia.

outside organs

bodily organs

outside organs Females' external genitalia are made up of The Clutians The pubic bone internal lips Outside lips the mouth of the uterus The term "vulva" refers to a woman's entire external genitalia. The vulva's appearance varies widely from woman to woman. The Aleutians The clitoris is a very delicate female sexual organ that extends deeper into the body and has a glans in front of the vaginal opening. It includes Glans. A tissue knob that is exterior to the urethral opening and vaginal opening fronds Perhaps an inch of the body is penetrated by a shaft made of two corpora cavernosa. Two longer, spongier bodies are buried deep within the body and extend from the clitoris tip to the main lips on either side of the vagina. Before birth, male and female sexual organs grow from the same tissue. Both the male penis and the female clitoris originate from the same embryonic tissue. The clitoris and penis both have corpora cavernosa, which is a structural similarity. The size of the clitoris varies from one woman to the next. It has an erectile clitoris. Similar to the corpora cavernosa in the penis, its interior anatomy has corpora cavernosa that fill with blood. The clitoris is extremely sensitive to touch because it contains a plentiful amount of nerve endings. The only component of the sexual anatomy with no known role in reproduction is this one. The fatty pad of tissue beneath the pubic hair is known as the Mons Mons pubis. The lateral exterior lips

Chapter Three

Gender Identity & Sexual Expression

Sexual expression, on the other hand, refers to how a person exhibits their gender, whether through behavior or outward appearance. Sexual identity relates to a person's feelings about their gender (such as their clothing or hairstyle). Others may identify as a different gender or as non-binary, while other people's gender identity corresponds to the sex they were given at birth.

A person's internal perception of their gender and sexual orientation is known as their sexual identity. Labels like gay, lesbian, bisexual, transgender and many others can fall under this category. The way a person publicly displays their gender and sexual orientation is referred to as sexual expression. How they present themselves, the pronouns they employ, and the individuals they engage in romantic and sexual interactions are a few examples. It's critical to keep in mind that there is no right or wrong way to be; instead, each person has their own sexual identity and expression. In terms of sexual identity and expression, it's critical to accept people's decisions and preferences.

The way a person identifies and presents their gender and sexuality is referred to as their sexual identity and expression. This can include their sexual orientation, their gender expression (how they display their gender through their appearance and behavior), and their gender identity (whether they identify as male, female, non-binary, etc). (who they are attracted to) An individual's sense of self in connection to their sexual orientation is referred to as their sexual identity. Labels like gay, lesbian, bisexual, or heterosexual, as well as more complicated identities that might not fall under these headings, can be included in this. Contrarily, sexual expression describes the various ways that a person chooses to exhibit their sexuality. This can involve acts, choices, and behaviors associated with relationships, desire, and sexual activity.

A person's perception of oneself as a sexual being is referred to as sexual identity. This can include their gender identity, sexual orientation, and method of sexual expression. Contrarily, sexual expression describes how a person communicates their sexuality and might include traits including behavior, appearance, and self-presentation. When someone self-identifies as straight, gay, lesbian, bisexual, transgender, etc., they are said to have a sexual identity. Sexual expression is the process by which a person reveals their sexual orientation and gender identity, which may be done through their actions, their appearance, or other means of self-expression. It's critical that people feel at ease and secure disclosing their sexual orientation and identity.

A person's internal sense of their gender and how they display it through their looks, conduct, and other traits are referred to as sexual identity and expression. This may take into account things like the gender that was assigned to them at birth, how they view themselves, and the way that they like to portray themselves to others.

A culture may define gender as a combination of socially constructed roles, attitudes, activities, and/or characteristics that it may deem appropriate for members of a specific sex. Like gender, gender identity refers to a person's subjective perception of being either male, female, or somewhere in between. The sex assumed or assigned at birth may or may not match gender identity. Gender expression, on the other hand, describes how a person displays their gender. This can include their names, pronouns, dress, and behaviors.

The list of commonly used gender identities and phrases is as follows:

A person who uses the word "agender" will frequently think of themselves as having no particular gender identification.

Cisgender: People who only identify with the gender assigned at birth are referred to as cisgender.

Demigender: This is a phrase used to describe someone who has an internal preference for one gender over another.
A person who transitions between genders easily or whose gender changes over time is referred to as gender flexible.

Someone who expresses themselves in a way that they don't want to be identified with any one gender is said to be gender neutral.

Gender nonconforming: The term "gender nonconforming" is most frequently used to refer to a gender expression that deviates from cultural gender norms or gender assigned at birth.

Genderqueer: The term "genderqueer" refers to a gender identity that isn't strictly male or female. Genderqueer persons have different experiences with their gender. Their identification may have aspects of the nonbinary, non-binary, and feminine, or none of these. It is possible to interpret genderqueer identity as a rejection of associations or labels.

One who is questioning all or some aspects of their gender identity or expression and does not want to identify as having a particular gender identity is said to be gender questioning.

Intergender: A gender identity that combines aspects of both masculine and feminine identities is referred to as intergender.

Multi-Gender: People who identify as more than one gender are said to be multi-gender.

A gender identity that cannot be classified as either masculine or feminine is known as nonbinary. Different gender experiences are had by nonbinary people. This identity may be perceived as a hybrid of male and female, as neither of the two or as something wholly unrelated to ideas of traditional gender identities.

Pangender: A person who identifies as all or many gender identities is said to be pangender.

Pronouns: Pronouns are quickly taking over as one of the most popular ways for people to specify their gender and how they prefer to be addressed. Respect requires the use of pronouns, yet they do not always reveal a person's gender identification. While a person who uses he/they pronouns may identify in a variety of ways, a person who uses she/her pronouns might nevertheless be nonbinary.

Transgender/Trans: The term "transgender" is used to identify anyone who identifies as a gender other than the one they were given at birth.

Chapter Four

Sexual Orientation

Straight, gay, or bisexual? A person's romantic and emotional inclination toward those of the same gender or a different gender is referred to as sexual orientation. A homosexual is someone who prefers to interact with other people of the same gender. A heterosexual individual has a sexual preference for people of the opposite gender. A person who identifies as bisexual has a sexual preference for both men and women. Some LGB people as well as some heterosexual people who like unorthodox sexual practices self-identify as queer. People's perceptions of you are affected by your sexual orientation. The idea that heterosexuality is the norm is known as heteronormativity. Attitudes Many people in America are against homosexuality. The unfavorable opinions are slowly shifting as a result of the LGBT liberation movement. Homophobia is a strong, irrational dread of homosexuals as well as unfavorable attitudes and behaviors toward them. Prejudice towards homosexuals and lesbians is referred to as antigay prejudice. The idea that heterosexuality is the norm and that everyone is heterosexual is known as heterosexism. Certain prejudices are subtle. Hate crimes committed against LGBs are when anti-gay prejudice is shown to its fullest extent. Physical, mental, and sexual harassment of sexual minorities is frequently coupled with hate crimes.

A person's emotional, physical, and sexual attraction to others of a particular gender is referred to as their sexual orientation. It is a term used to define a person's sexual orientation, which is commonly classified as gay, lesbian, bisexual, or straight. It's crucial to understand that gender identity, which relates to a person's internal sense of their gender, is distinct from sexual orientation.
A person's emotional, physical, and sexual attraction to other people is referred to as

their sexual orientation. It may be directed against those who are of the same gender (homosexual), those who are of the opposite gender (heterosexual), or both (bisexual). Some people may also describe themselves as pansexual, which means they are drawn to people regardless of how they identify as gendered. It is a crucial component of one's identity and has an impact on how one relates to people and their environment. A person's emotional, romantic, and sexual attraction to others of a particular gender or sex is referred to as their sexual orientation. This can involve a preference for people of a certain gender (homosexuality), the same gender (heterosexuality), or different genders (bisexuality). A person's sexual orientation is a crucial component of who they are and is not something they can choose.

Who you are attracted to and want to be in relationships with determines your sexual orientation. Gay, lesbian, straight, bisexual, and asexual is the different sexual orientations.

Gender and gender identity are distinct from sexual orientation.
Sexual orientation refers to the people you are emotionally, romantically, and sexually drawn to. It's not the same as gender identity. Gender identification refers to who you ARE – male, female, genderqueer, etc. – rather than who you are attracted to.

As a result, being transgender—feeling as though the gender you identify with is very different from the sex you were assigned—is distinct from being gay, lesbian, or bisexual. What matters in sexual orientation is who you want to be with. The question of gender identity is personal.

Numerous identities are connected to sexual orientation, including:

People who are attracted to a different gender, such as men or women who are drawn to women, may identify as straight or heterosexual.

The terms "gay" or "homosexual" are frequently used by people who are attracted to other people of the same gender. Lesbians may be preferred by gay women.

People who have feelings for both men and women frequently identify as bisexuals.

Pansexual or queer individuals are those who find themselves attracted to people of many different gender identities, including male, female, transgender, genderqueer, intersex, etc.

People who are unsure about their sexual orientation may describe themselves as curious or unsure.

Those who don't feel any sexual desire toward someone commonly identify as asexuals.

Also noteworthy is the fact that some individuals feel none of these designations adequately describe them. Some people have strong opposition to the concept of labels. Some designations are acceptable to some people while not others. You get to choose how if at all, you wish to label yourself.

Queer: What does that mean?
Diverse sexual orientations and gender identities that are not straight and cisgender are referred to as queer.

The term "queer" was once used to injure and deride others. Some people still find it insulting, especially those who are still sensitive to the way the word was once used. Others now proudly self-identify with the word.

If you don't know how they identify themselves, you might not want to call them "queer." Use their language while discussing their sexual orientation with others. Asking about people's preferred labels is acceptable (and frequently encouraged!).

Asexuality: What is it?
Asexual people don't experience sexual attraction to anyone. They may find other individuals to be physically alluring or desire romantic connections with them, but they are not interested in engaging in sexual activity with them. Asexual people occasionally abbreviate words with "ace."

The romantic attraction has nothing to do with asexuality. Many asexual people experience romantic attraction toward others, leading them to self-identify as both asexual and homosexual, lesbian, bisexual, or straight. They simply lack the willingness to act sexually on these feelings.

Like everyone else, asexual folks have emotional needs. While some asexuals are interested in romantic relationships, others are not. Other than sex, they establish intimacy or closeness with others.

Some individuals who identify as aromantic do not experience romantic attraction or desire romantic partnerships. Being asexual and being aromantic are two different things.

While some asexuals are aroused (turned on), they lack the desire to engage in sexual activity with others. Also, some asexuals engage in masturbation. Others, however, might not experience any arousal at all.

Even though it's very natural to have periods when you don't want to have sex, this does not necessarily indicate that you are an asexual. Asexuality is not the same as celibacy, either. Asexuality is a sexual identity that comes naturally to you, whereas celibacy is a decision you make.

Asexuality, like other sexual orientations, isn't usually clear-cut. Between being sexual (having a sexual desire) and being asexual, there is a range. Individuals fall into several categories throughout that spectrum. Some people who don't find other people sexually attractive identify as gray-a. Some persons who only experience sexual attraction to others with whom they are in committed relationships self-identify as demisexual. Interested in learning how someone identifies? Query them.

There is nothing "wrong" with persons who are asexual, and there is no proof that this is due to poor mental health or trauma of any type. According to some studies, one out of every 100 adults is asexual.

What influences sexual preference?
The reasons behind someone's lesbian, gay, straight, or bisexual orientation are not fully understood. However, studies suggest that biological variables that begin before birth may have a role in the development of sexual orientation.

People don't choose who they are attracted to, and neither counseling nor other forms of persuasion can alter someone's sexual orientation. A person cannot be "turned" gay either. For instance, exposing a boy to dolls or other toys that are typically meant for girls won't make him gay.

You probably become aware of your attraction to some people at a very young age. Just because you could recognize persons you thought were attractive or liked them does not imply that you had sexual impulses for them. Many claims that they were aware of their sexual orientation even before they reached puberty.

Although sexual orientation is typically determined early in infancy, it's not unusual for your preferences and attractor patterns to change throughout your lifetime. We refer to this as "fluidity." Many people, including scientists and sex researchers, think that sexual orientation is like a scale, with the completely gay end and the completely straight end. Many people prefer to be in the middle rather than the extremes.

How numerous are LGBTQ people?
Lesbian, Gay, Bisexual, Transgender, and Questioning is referred to as LGBTQ.

Although researchers make an effort to determine the number of LGBTQ people, it is quite challenging to obtain an exact figure. This is due to the complexity of people's gender identification, sexual orientation, sexual identity, and sexual behavior. Let's deconstruct it:

Your internal gender identity determines how you express yourself externally through your actions, words, and clothing, among other things.

The emotional or sexual feelings you have for someone else are known as sexual attraction.

You identify yourself by your sexual orientation (for example, using labels such as queer, gay, lesbian, straight, or bisexual).

Sexual behavior refers to the people you have sex with and the types of sex you enjoy.

Sometimes a person can have all of these things. For instance, a woman might only be attracted to other women, identity as a lesbian, and only have intercourse with other women.

However, these factors don't always coincide. Not everyone who feels attracted to someone of the same gender will act on those feelings. Even if they may act in same-gender sexual ways, some persons may not self-identify as bisexual, lesbian, or homosexual. Not everyone feels comfortable coming out as LGBTQ since in some circumstances doing so can lead to fear and persecution. Some people's sexual orientation and the labels they use to describe themselves can change throughout their lives.

The complexity of sexual orientation and gender for so many people makes it challenging to estimate the number of LGBTQ people. And not everyone feels secure or at ease disclosing their sexual orientation to someone else.

According to recent studies, only 3.5% of American people identify as lesbian, gay, or bisexual, although 11% of them admit to feeling at least some same-sex attraction, and 8.2% admit to engaging in same-sex conduct. This demonstrates how people's actions and feelings are not always consistent with how they define themselves. How can I tell what my sexual preference is? Not everyone is aware of their sexual orientation or how to identify it in this section. You're not alone if you feel this way; it's a common feeling.

What happens if I'm not certain about my sexual orientation?
This is typical, and it doesn't indicate that you have any health issues. Understanding one's sexual orientation might take years or even a lifetime for some people. People frequently discover that they have been "questioning" for some time or that none of the categories used to categorize sexual orientation apply to them.

Some individuals could test a label to see whether it fits before switching to a different one if it doesn't. This is also alright. You are not required to choose just one label, and it is acceptable if your current feelings change in the future.

Some people have difficulty coming out to others or even to themselves because they worry about homophobia and discrimination based on sexual orientation. Many LGBTQ persons deal with these difficulties daily.

If you ever wondered, "Am I homosexual or bisexual?" It's not just you. You might be able to solve the problem by speaking to a dependable friend or family member.

Can others infer my sexual orientation from me?
No. Only you may reveal your sexual preference to another person. Only you know how you feel on the inside; your sexual orientation expresses that.

Some people can believe that they can determine someone's sexual orientation by looking at them, how they dress, or how they act. These are fairly generalized assumptions about how lesbian, gay, and bisexual people behave. But just like heterosexuals, homosexual and bisexual individuals can seem, behave, and dress in a variety of ways. It can be misleading and cruel to categorize someone else's sexual orientation using stereotypes.

"Coming out" is what?

Not everybody emerges in the same manner. Additionally, not everyone comes out to everyone in their life at the same time or comes out to everyone. There is no one way to exit that is correct.

What does the phrase "coming out" mean?

When someone who identifies as LGBTQ works to accept their sexual orientation or gender identity and communicate it freely with other people, they are said to be coming out.

It takes a lot of courage to come out, and everyone experiences it differently. When you come out, you could feel everything from afraid and apprehensive to thrilled and relieved.

There is no one way to exit that is correct. There are many things to think about before coming out, but it can sometimes feel better to be upfront and honest about your sexual orientation than to hide it.

It takes time to come out. Coming out to oneself is frequently the first step. This occurs as you become aware of and start to embrace your sexual orientation. Then, you might decide to inform your family, friends, and neighbors – sometimes immediately, sometimes later. With some people in your life, you could choose to be completely honest.
Being out is a lifelong process. Coming out is a continuous struggle because many

individuals assume that everyone they encounter is heterosexual. An LGBTQ-identified individual must choose whether, when, and how to come out to new acquaintances (friends, coworkers, nurses, and medical professionals, for example).

The decision to come out depends on the circumstances. The process of coming out can be liberating and can help you get closer to the people you care about. But it can also be stressful, even harmful or risky. In some circumstances, it could feel safer for you to remain hidden. You do not need to be outside constantly. Which option is ideal for you is up to you.

There can be advantages and risks to coming out. There are several factors to take into account if you're debating coming out. Does coming out mean you run the danger of losing your family's financial or emotional support? Could you put yourself in harm's way by coming out? Will your family make an effort to persuade you to change who you are? If the answer to any of these was "yes," you might want to postpone your decision until you have more support or are in a new circumstance.

Your experience of coming out is entirely up to you. Your decision regarding how, when, where, and with whom to be open about your sexual orientation is entirely up to you (and your gender identity). Starting by being upfront with someone who shares your sexual orientation or gender identity may seem safer. This might occur online, in community centers, at a club or group for LGBTQ people, or with a select group of close friends.

How can I tell my parents and friends that I'm gay?
There is no one, ideal approach to telling your family and friends that you are gay or lesbian. You know best what feels

appropriate to you and whom you should confide in.

Here are some ideas to help the talk go more smoothly:

Give yourself some time to prepare your approach and your speech before you determine that you're ready to step out.

Choose the individuals in your life who you believe will react to the news the least negatively and start with them. How someone responds when the subject of LGBTQ persons is brought up in conversation is frequently a good indicator of how accepting they are of them.

Do some study to provide yourself with knowledge about LGBTQ people in case your loved one has inquiries or is unaware of the realities.

Instead of informing someone in person, you might feel better at ease coming out in a letter or email. It's OK.

Be ready to wait as they process and accept the new information when you pick who to come out to, what to say to them, and how to say it. Allow them the space they require.

Approach the situation with an open mind rather than assuming that everyone would react negatively. Many individuals already know other LGBTQ persons in their lives, and you might be surprised by some people's openness and acceptance.